EARTHWISE

Sun

Jim Pipe

Stargazer Books

CONTENTS

© Aladdin Books Ltd 2005

First published in the
United States in 2005 by:
Stargazer Books
c/o The Creative Company
123 South Broad Street
P.O. Box 227
Mankato, Minnesota 56002

All rights reserved

Design
Flick, Book Design
and Graphics

Educational Consultant
Jackie Holderness

Picture Research
Brian Hunter Smart

Printed in U.A.E.

Library of Congress
Cataloging-in-Publication Data

Pipe, Jim, 1966-
    Sun / by Jim Pipe.
        p. cm.-- (Earthwise)
    Includes index.
    ISBN 1-932799-46-X (alk paper)
    1. Sun--Juvenile literature.
    I. Title. II. Series.

QB521.5.P57 2004
523.7--dc22   2004040197

INTRODUCTION

From Earth, the sun looks like a bright, round disk in the sky. It is actually our nearest star, a swirling mass of hot gases spinning around in space. The sun sends out a stream of energy that warms and lights the earth. Without this, our planet would be cold and lifeless.

HOW TO USE THIS BOOK

Watch for the symbol of the magnifying glass for tips on how to observe the world around you.

The paintbrush boxes contain an activity you can do that is related to the sun.

OUR NEAREST STAR

The sun is our local star. It is just like many of the other stars you see in the sky at night. Yet, because it is so much closer to us, the sun is more important to us than anything else in the sky. Without the sun's heat and light, there could be no life on Earth.

It is **NEVER** safe to look directly at the sun, even when it is low in the sky.

Many ancient peoples believed the sun was a god and built temples to honor it. Ancient buildings such as Stonehenge in England (below) may also have been used to record the position of the sun during the year.

The sun affects the earth in many important ways. It is the source of all our energy, and its heat influences our weather. It gives us our nights and days, seasons, and years.

Sun Paintings

How would you paint the sun? You can paint it as a round disk with lines to show its rays. You can show sunlight by painting shadows or showing how light shines into a dark room. See how different artists show the beauty and warmth of the sun in these paintings.

The Love Letter (left) by Jan Vermeer van Delft

Yosemite Valley (above) by Albert Berstadt

The sun is a round disk in this ancient Egyptian painting.

THE STORMY SUN

Like other stars, the sun is a huge, glowing ball of gas. About five billion years ago, a thick cloud of dust and gas began to pull together to form a globe. As it squashed together, the cloud got thicker and hotter.

Finally, it got so hot that parts of it began to explode. Luckily for us, these explosions have never stopped: they make the sun shine!

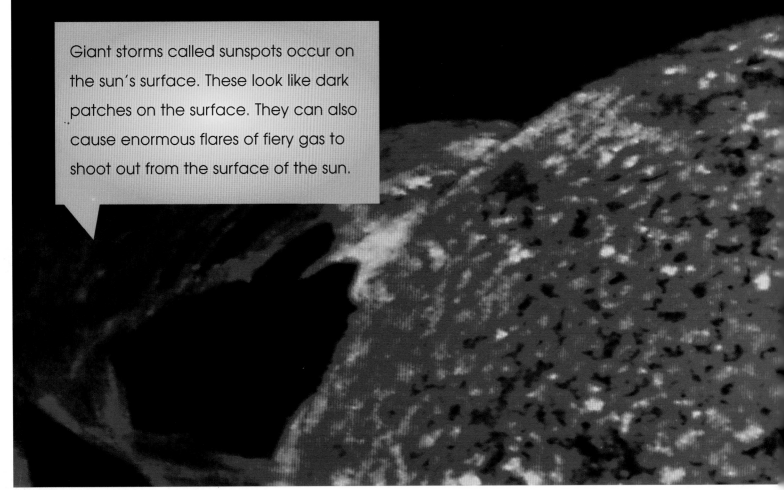

Giant storms called sunspots occur on the sun's surface. These look like dark patches on the surface. They can also cause enormous flares of fiery gas to shoot out from the surface of the sun.

AURORAS

If you live in a region near the North or South poles, the sun puts on an amazing light show. Clouds and streaks of color, called auroras, light up the sky at night (right). They are caused by electricity from the sun. Some are thousands of miles long.

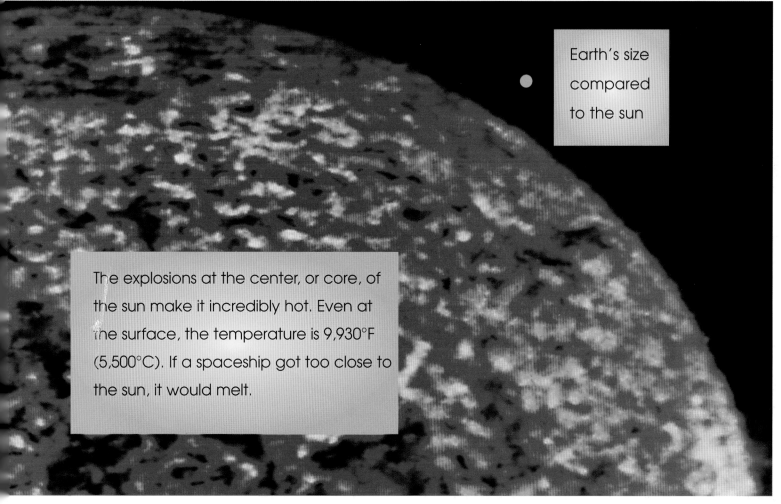

Earth's size compared to the sun

The explosions at the center, or core, of the sun make it incredibly hot. Even at the surface, the temperature is 9,930°F (5,500°C). If a spaceship got too close to the sun, it would melt.

THE SOLAR SYSTEM

As the sun was being born, planets began to form from the gas and dust that circled it. The planets are still traveling around the sun, including our planet, Earth.

The sun is about 93 million miles from us. Our fastest spacecraft can travel at about 25,000 miles per hour. If it could go at this speed all the way, a trip to the sun would take over 150 days.

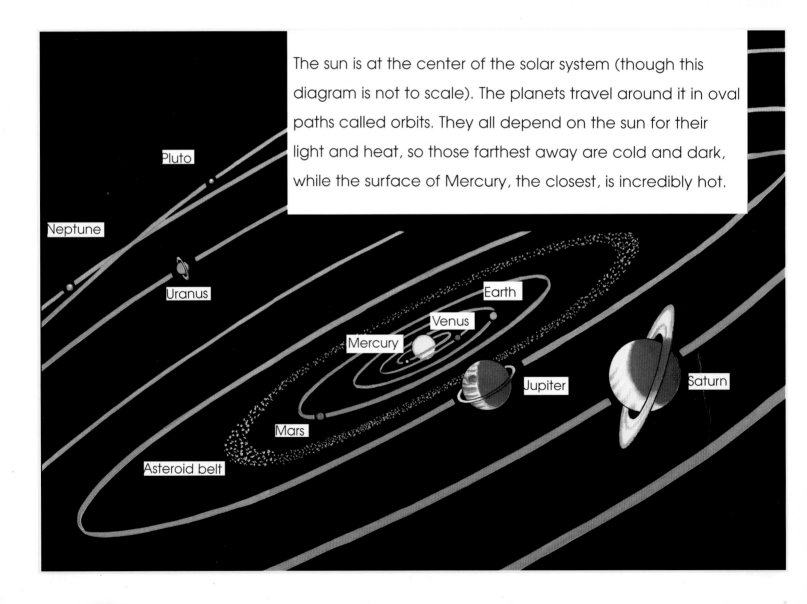

The sun is at the center of the solar system (though this diagram is not to scale). The planets travel around it in oval paths called orbits. They all depend on the sun for their light and heat, so those farthest away are cold and dark, while the surface of Mercury, the closest, is incredibly hot.

Pluto

Neptune

Uranus

Earth

Venus

Mercury

Jupiter

Saturn

Mars

Asteroid belt

Sun Display

Compare the different sizes of the planets in the solar system using the following items. Take a beach ball for the sun (right), then line up the planets using peppercorns for Mercury and Mars, dried peas for Venus and Earth, an orange for Jupiter, a tangerine for Saturn, walnuts for Uranus and Neptune, and a grain of rice for Pluto. To remember the planet order, think: Many Varied Experiments Make Jolly Scientists Unusually Noisy People!

MILKY • WAY

The sun is just one of billions of stars in the Milky Way galaxy. While the earth takes a year to circle the sun, the sun takes about 200 million years to make one circle around the center of the Milky Way.

You can see parts of the Milky Way on clear, dark nights. It looks like a milky band of starlight stretching across the sky.

SUNLIGHT

The sun shines like an enormous flashlight beam through the darkness of space. Only a tiny part of its light reaches us. The rest is lost in space. But this is still more than enough to fill our world with light—the sun is the source of all our natural light.

On Earth, sunlight looks white (left), but it actually contains all the colors of the rainbow. These colors mix to form white sunlight. Without sunlight we wouldn't see any colors. That is why everything looks black at night.

Rainbows

When you paint a rainbow, you need lots of colors! Rainbows appear when the sun shines through raindrops. The sunlight bounces off the raindrops and splits into the seven colors of the rainbow (right).

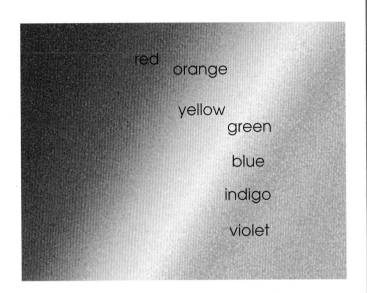

red
orange
yellow
green
blue
indigo
violet

Mellow • Glow

At sunrise or sunset, the sun turns orange or red and fills the sky with warm, hazy light. When the sun is this low in the sky, its light has to travel through a thicker layer of air. So, more of its rays are scattered by tiny dust particles and drops of water in the air.

Light from the sun reaches the other planets in the solar system. For example, Mars has no air, but dust particles in its atmosphere make the sky look red! If you stood on Mars, you might see pink clouds of dust in addition to blue and white clouds made up of ice or water droplets.

NIGHT AND DAY

We talk about sunrise, but the sun doesn't really rise at all. It just looks like it does because the earth is like a spinning ball. Wherever you live, it gets light as your part of the earth turns to face the sun. The sun's light makes the sky grow brighter and morning begins. The earth keeps spinning and the sun seems to move across the sky.

Toward evening, your part of the earth is turning away from the sun. The sun seems to sink down and it gets dark. Now it's night!

Sunrise and Sunset

Use a compass (right) to find out where the sun rises and sets. If you try in winter, you won't have to get up so early! Line up the needle so that it is pointing to N for north. With the needle in this position, the letters E, S, and W point to east, south, and west. You should find that the sun rises in the east and sets in the west.

TWILIGHT

Have you noticed how the sky is still light for a while just before sunrise or just after sunset? These times of day are called twilight. The sun is below the horizon, but its light can still be seen because its rays are scattered by the earth's atmosphere.

In space, the sun is always shining (below), so there is no day or night. Some astronauts wear blindfolds to shut out the sun when they want to sleep.

THE MOON

The moon is a dark mass of rock that circles the earth, but it looks bright because one side is always lit by the sun. So, moonlight is actually sunlight that is bouncing off the moon.

At full moon, the sun lights up one whole side of the moon. In early calendars, one month was the time between two full moons, or 29½ days.

Moon Shapes

As the moon moves around the earth, the sun lights it up from different directions so that it seems to change shape (left).

Draw the shape of the moon once every few days to see how it changes from a full moon to a new moon (when the moon's dark side is facing the earth).

E CLIPSES

Once or twice a year, part, or the whole of the sun is blocked out as the moon passes between it and the earth (right). This is a solar eclipse. In a lunar eclipse, the moon darkens as the earth passes between it and the sun.

OUR SUN CLOCK

Since ancient times, people have used the sun to keep track of time. The time between sunrise and sunset gives us our day (top). The time it takes the earth to make one complete orbit around the sun gives us our year, which is 365 1/4 days long. Ancient peoples also used sundials (page 17) to measure the day in hours.

TIME • ZONES

Around the world, clocks are set at different times so that everyone awakes as it gets light and goes to sleep when it is dark. So, when it is 1pm, or lunchtime, in New York, it is 6pm, or dinnertime in England.

Sundials

On sunny days you can tell the time using a sundial. Place a stick in the ground and mark where its shadow falls at 10am.

Return each hour and mark where the stick's shadow is with a stone. The next day you can tell the time by seeing which stone the shadow points to.

In summer, the sun climbs higher in the sky than it does in winter. Because of this, your shadow is usually much longer in winter (left) than it is in summer (above).

THE WEATHERMAKER

The sun is the driving force behind our weather. Sunlight heats up some parts of the earth more than others, making the air warmer above these areas. This warm air moves about, causing wind and changes in the weather. Heat from the sun also turns water in the air into clouds, rain, and snow.

SEASONS

The seasons are caused by the way that the earth moves around the sun. In summer, your half of the world is nearer the sun, so it is hotter. In winter, your half is farther away, so it is colder. With each season, the changes in weather affect plants and animals. Look for blossom or fresh shoots in spring, bees and butterflies in summer, and tumbling leaves in fall.

Winter

Spring

Fall

Summer

Sunny Days and Blue Skies

When the sun is high in the sky, some of its blue light rays are scattered in the air above us. This makes the sky look blue and the sun appear yellow.

Wind

The sun's heat warms the air, causing it to rise. Then, cold air moves in to replace the warm air. This movement of air is what we call wind.

Clouds

When heat from the sun warms the air, it rises up into the sky, where it cools. As it cools, water vapor (gas) in the air turns into millions of tiny water droplets that gather together into clouds.

Rain and Snow

Heat from the sun turns water from the sea's surface into a gas, called water vapor. This rises high into the sky, where it cools and turns into drops of water that fall to the ground as rain. If the air is very cold, the water in clouds turns to snow.

SUN SAFETY

When the sun shines on you it feels wonderful, but you need to be careful. An invisible part of sunlight, called ultraviolet (UV) light, can harm your skin and your eyes. Even when you are in the shade, the ground can reflect harmful UV light onto you.

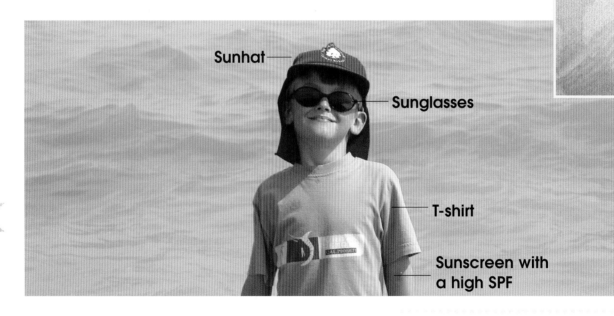

Sunhat

Sunglasses

T-shirt

Sunscreen with a high SPF

NEVER look into the sun. To protect your eyes, wear sunglasses with UV protection (top). If you are playing on a beach or in the water, be sure to cover up with a light-colored T-shirt. You should also wear a wide hat, as too much sun can give you a bad headache or make you feel sick.

SUNSCREENS

Sunscreens can protect your skin from the sun. If you look closely at them, their sun protection factor (SPF) tells you how strong they are.

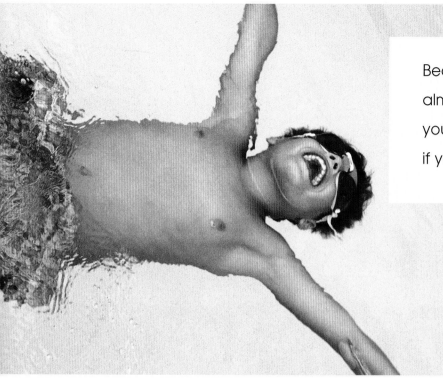

Because it reflects the sunlight, water can almost double the amount of sun that hits you. So, you have to be especially careful if you are in the water or out on a boat.

Don't rely on sunscreens too much. On a very hot day, stay inside or in the shade (right) when the sun is at its strongest, between 10am and 4pm.

For example, when you put on an SPF 2 sunscreen, it takes twice as long for your skin to become sunburned. A good sunscreen should be at least 15 SPF, even if you are just sitting in the shade.

It is best to put on sun creams or lotions at least 20 minutes before you go out into the sun.

LIGHT FOR LIFE

The steady flow of light and heat from the sun keeps our planet warm and enables plants to make food.

Apart from bacteria living in rocks far below the ground, almost all animals on Earth depend on the sun for food. If the sun ever cooled, the earth would become cold and lifeless.

The earth is just the right distance away from the sun. If it were as close to the sun as Venus is, the earth would be too hot for most plants and animals.

Likewise, if the earth were as far away from the sun as Jupiter (right) is, it would probably be too cold to support anything but the toughest life forms.

SUNFLOWERS

You may think that sunflowers (right) get their name from looking like bright yellow suns. However, they are called sunflowers for another reason.

As the sun rises in the morning, sunflowers turn to face it. As the sun moves throughout the day, the sunflowers turn their heads to follow it across the sky. The next time you pass a field of sunflowers, notice which way they are all facing!

Plants and animals are part of what we call the food chain. Almost all food chains start with green plants that use energy from sunlight and water from the soil to make food. Grass, for example, is eaten by planteaters such as antelopes, which are in turn eaten by lions (above).

Without the sun feeding the grass, neither of these animals would survive.

Bean Race

You can test how important sunlight is to a growing plant. Plant two bean seeds (right) in different pots. Leave one pot in a sunny place, and the other the shade. If you water them equally, the plant in the sun should grow much faster.

ANIMALS AND THE SUN

All animals need the sun to survive. It provides them with food, light, and warmth. It can even help them to find food. When a bee finds food, it returns to its hive and uses a dance to tell the other bees where the food is in relation to the sun's position.

Birds like the Arctic tern (above), fly long distances in search of food or a place to nest. They may use the sun or the stars to find their way.

It is hard for a large animal like a rhinoceros to keep cool in the sun. But a roll in the mud can help (left)!

Like all reptiles, this lizard (right) uses the sun to keep its body at the right temperature. After a cold night, it lies out in the sun to warm up. When it gets too hot, it crawls into the shade to cool down.

Many animals rely on the sun's heat and light during the day. But some hunters go to work just as the sun is going down. Wolves (right) and lions have excellent senses of smell and hearing that allow them to hunt in low light. Bats (above) feed on moths and other insects at night while most birds are asleep.

ENERGY FROM THE SUN

The sun is our most important source of heat, which is why it is colder at night when our side of the world is in shadow. Without the sun's heat, we would soon freeze.

Heat and light from the sun also provide almost all of our planet's energy needs. Every 40 minutes, the sun delivers as much energy to the earth's surface as all the people on Earth use in a year.

SOLAR • CELLS

Do you know someone with a fountain (right), or a calculator powered by solar energy cells? These turn the sun's heat into electricity. Unlike burning oil, gas, or coal, solar cells cause no pollution. However, scientists are looking for ways to make them cheaper and more efficient.

The sun's fuel is a gas called hydrogen. Though it has already been shining for five billion years, the sun has enough hydrogen left to carry on shining for at least another five billion years.

One day the sun will die, however. It will slowly swell to become a giant red star and then cool down and fade away.

The sun's energy is stored in plants and animals. This energy can be used in a variety of ways. For example, trees can be burned as firewood. When we burn coal, oil, or natural gas (below), the sun's energy is released after being stored in fossils millions of years ago.

Solar Energy

Solar cells (below right) are just one way of using the sun's energy. Solar furnaces heat water by using lots of mirrors to focus sunlight onto one point. To see how this is done, try reflecting sunlight onto the same point on a wall using a small mirror in each hand. The sun also causes wind, so it provides the wind energy that windfarms (above right) turn into electricity.

OUR FRIENDLY SUN

In addition to giving us the light, heat, and energy we need to live, the shining sun often puts us in a good mood. Lots of activities are more fun on a sunny day. But if the sky is gray, remember that above the clouds, the sun is always shining!

Sunny Days

There are lots of songs that mention the sun. Many of them are about feeling happy. How do you feel on a sunny day? Write your own story, song, or poem, using the sun to describe your feelings.

Mellow Lazy Warm Hot Hazy HAPPY Glowing Bright YELLOW

In winter, regions near the poles don't have any sun for several months. The tilt of the earth means that the sun never rises above the horizon.

However, during the summer months (left) the sun is out all day—and all night. So, you can read a book outside at midnight!

In northern regions, where winter days are short and dark, some people miss the sun so much that they feel ill. Doctors call this Seasonal Affective Disorder (SAD). Bright lights are sometimes used to treat sufferers.

Rise • And • Shine!

Have you ever heard birds singing loudly just as the sun rises? This is the dawn chorus, the sound of male birds singing. They compete by singing as loud as they can. When a rooster crows at dawn, it is showing off to the hens, not trying to wake you up!

USEFUL WORDS

atmosphere—the air that surrounds the earth, or the mix of gases that surrounds any planet.

aurora—glowing streaks of light that appear in the northern or southern sky when electricity from the sun hits the earth's atmosphere.

eclipse—when one object in space moves in front of another to block its light. A solar eclipse takes place when the sun appears to become dark as the moon passes between the sun and the earth.

fossil fuels—coal, oil, and gas, formed from the fossils of prehistoric plants and animals that have trapped energy from the Sun.

galaxy—a group of billions of stars and solar systems. Our solar system is in the Milky Way galaxy.

moonlight—light from the sun that bounces off the moon.

seasons—the regular changes in temperature and weather that happen every year at about the same time.

solar cells—units containing chemicals that turn sunlight into electricity.

solar system—the sun and all the planets and their moons that orbit around it.

star—a huge ball of hot gas that shines because of the energy created in explosions at its core.

sun protection factor (SPF)—the higher its SPF number, the longer a sunscreen or sun lotion protects your skin from sunburn.

sunspots—storms on the sun's surface that appear darker than the rest of its surface.

temperature—how hot or cold something is, usually measured in degrees of Fahrenheit or Centigrade.

ultraviolet (UV) light—the invisible rays in sunlight that can cause sunburn.

Find Out More

Take a look at these books & websites:

Books:
Science World: Solar System
(Stargazer Books)

Websites:
www.kidsastronomy.com
www.museum.vic.gov.au/planetarium
www.artyastro.com/artyend.htm

MELTDOWN

Test the melting power of the sun by putting cubes of butter in two bowls and a few ice cubes in two similar bowls. Put one bowl of each item in the hot sun and place the other two bowls in the shade. Every ten minutes, check all the bowls. You should find that the butter and ice melt a lot faster in the sun.

INDEX

Photocredits

Abbreviations: l-left, r-right, b-bottom, t-top, c-center, m-middle

Front cover tr & br, 1, 5ml, 10-11, 12tr, 14-15, 18tl, 18mr, 18bm, 18br, 23tr, 24ml, 24br, 25 both, 28mr — Digital Stock. Front cover tl, bl & c, 2-3, 4-5, 6-7, 7tr, 9br, 11 all, 13, 14bl, 15 both, 19ml, 21tl, 26tl, 26-27, 29t, 30-31 — Corbis. Front cover inset, 9tr, 12br, 17tr, 20c, 21b, 22br, 23br, 26br — Flick Smith. Back cover, 27mr, 28br — Comstock. 3b — Julian Cox. 5c, 5mr, 5br, 16 both — Corel. 6tl, 8tl, 14tl, 24tr — Stockbyte. 10bl, 17mr, 17bl, 18c, 21mr, 30bl — Digital Vision. 19mr, 19bm, 27tr, 27br, 28ml, 31bl, 32b — Photodisc. 23tl — NASA. 28tr — Image 100. 29br — John Foxx Images.